CARNIVOROUS

Moyra Donaldson

Doire Press

First published in 2019

Doire Press
Aille, Inverin
Co. Galway
www.doirepress.com

Layout: Lisa Frank
Cover design: Tríona Walsh
Cover photo: Witaya Ratanasirikulchai / Dreamstime.com
Author photo: Donna Rowley

Printed by Clódóirí CL
Casla, Co. na Gaillimhe

ISBN 978-1-907682-68-1

We gratefully acknowledge the assistance of The Arts Council of Northern Ireland.

LOTTERY FUNDED

CONTENTS

for the animals

Nature

Yesterday, three swallow chicks,
today, one magpie.
Tonight an empty nest.

Each Year I Do the Fence

Hour after long hour; creosote,
brush, repetitive movement

along the horizontal length
of it, then up and down
the planted vertical

that keeps it standing,
interstices of sky and earth and time:

preserving the planks,
stopping the posts from rotting,
keeping the space intact.

I like to step back occasionally, count
the sections done and those still

to be done, all the time knowing
that when it is finished
it will need done again.

Eventually there's no finesse to it,
no artistry except persistence

and what each year brings
cannot all be mended, there's
algae, splitting, looseness —
I tie back my hair and get on.

A Quare Few Things

Over a lifetime, the gods
make many things of you.

One terrible winter, I was an iris.
Oh do not assume that bulbs
remember spring and flowering.

I've sat down at a table laid
with the corpse of my child
and been expected to eat.

And I have soared of course,
seen how the world is spread
wide for those who fly. I have
killed with beak and talons
to fill the little gaping throats.

I have asked for the chariot's reins
and set my whole world blazing.

I have been fox and snake and bear.
I have been stone and waterfall.
I have been loved too much and not enough.
I have been split open by the first green shoot.
I have been folded neat and safe inside my shell.
I have been both grit and pearl.
I have been the earth's gold veins,
the aching rift between the continents.

I have been a hart, hunted
through the darkening woods;
and the heart pierced by arrows,
chambers breached and flooded.
I was the vanishing point too.

Black Dream Bird

It was yesterday
that I was a crow
with horse hair in my beak
and my nest half built
and my black feathers
shining through the early mist
of belonging to the world
of knowing how to balance
on the air of the world
and my shadow
the same colour as myself.

Even when the farmer
tied my body lifeless
to the wire in warning
and my bones poked out
still I flapped in the wind
and raised my wings,
my beak hinged open
to the call of the air.

Thin

Wing of collar bone,
concavity between
the sculptural jut of hips,
trilobite processes of spine,
cage of ribs; and love,
the hungry prisoner.

Drumhirk Farm: All Souls' Night

My sleeping mother is very young
and very old; on the wall above
her sleeping head are butterflies,
their gold wings folded, but for one,
bright blue, with trembling wings extended.

There is no one left alive now in this house,
so I pick my sleeping mother up to take her
somewhere else; light as a sackful of feathers
in my arms, she is no burden as we move down
the dark green lanes, between hawthorn hedges,
fields where shadow shapes of cattle raise
their heads to mark our passing, and the moon's
reflection shines as understanding in their eyes:
it is long ago and now, never and forever.

My Mother's Coat

I don't remember her wearing it,
there's not even a photograph.
I don't know how she afforded it
on her teacher's salary and my father
a booking office clerk for the railways
who brought his wages home
in a brown envelope on a Friday night.
It was a film star's item of clothing,
with its mink collar —

at least that's how I remember it,
hanging in the wardrobe,
smelling of mothballs, heavy as a quilt
when I'd secretly take it from its hanger
and slip my adolescent self into it,
feeling the silk lining against arms and legs,
folding it around my body, caressing
the tight unyielding curls,
black and shiny, almost alien, something
unnatural seeping through the glamour,
a darkness felt in the heart; a repellent attraction.
I wondered what sort of animal had a coat like that.

In the days after the funeral, my sister-in-law
threw it out with all the other stuff
or I'd have kept it.
It takes the pelts of thirty lambs
to make one Persian Lamb coat.
They must be under three days old,
ideally foetal,
so as to have that deep blackness,
those most desirable close curls.

Morning Questions

Carried through the night
in a fist of dreams,
emptied into the light.

Rain comes down;
the water level rises.
Are you drowned, Mother?

Is this your face
beneath the surface?
Blemished and bloated.

Is the May blossom out
and I've not noticed?

Are you still
disappointed in me?

The Sixtieth Year of Horror Stories

When I was young I loved to scare myself
with stories read beneath the blankets
late at night by the light of a torch,
curse of the monkey's paw,
the haunted doll's house,
weight of a cat on the end of the bed
when you know there's no cat there.

Now all the what-ifs follow me about,
sit on my chest, restrict my breath;
the late-night phone call; blue lights;
the knock at the door; the cocked gun
of my children's lives pressed to my temple
day in day out; the diagnosis; the unlatched
gate — horses escaping into the night;
the hooked beak of grief: now it's real.

Memory

That night when the bats
buzzed us, close enough
for us to feel the soft draught
of their passing; that night
so thick with darkness
that we could see nothing.

Coming out of Winter

When I told the young GP I'd always been prone to melancholy,
she looked at me strangely, it's not a word for which
she has a prescription; but here, now, today, the sun is shining
and I have showered and washed my hair and I'm carrying on
moment to moment as she advised and I have plans
to plant some flowers and preciously waste some time
by looking out the window at the buzzard on her high tree
and at the bright blaze of gorse and the beginning of greening.
Though the May's not out, so I won't cast a clout just yet.

In the Year of Not Caring

I discovered that I like my body even yet,
how it opens into itself in the light.
I remembered all of it, concavity,
convexity, bones and skin and heart.

I still wanted some thunderous justice,
some knife to the guts of them, some
deadly blow, though I made efforts
to show kindness, to keep
my judgements to myself.

I discovered an old book of longing;
a list that keeps growing.
I wasn't one person and never had been.
I talked myself out of things.

I still wanted some bell-like truth
ringing. I wanted the spirits to reveal
themselves and speak clearly for once;
ghosts of starvation, of blood, walking
the streets of the town, crying.

We were Speaking and then the Bright Half-Moon and Jupiter

A black volcanic bowl
with one blue stream across
and a jug that holds no water.

Architect drawings are fading
and each morning now the house
has rearranged itself.
Through which window
will the sun rise today?
On what will it set?

The word is written on the wall
by a mysterious hand.
See how it shines above your head,
as if it was the word of god,
as if the word was out that you can hate
as well as you can love, or better;
yes, word is out, word is on the street.
Kneel down for it and do not blink.

In the Rothko Room

Black on maroon, red on maroon.

Sitting here in silence
you could believe in soul.
Or something like it —

some connection to the universe
that comes in through the eyes;
vibrates to sternum, guts, marrow.

You find yourself crying —
having that connection, you know
how unconnected you have been.

Signs and Wonders

A small feather
curl from a crow
floats down dark
against washed out
pale evening sky
and the faint idea
of a new moon

lands at my feet.

Hamilton Road Presbyterian 1964

Because there was God but also Jesus and the Holy Spirit,
it seemed the sermon also had to have three (long) parts:
three always added up to one exquisite boredom on a Sunday.

Stylistically embroidered, a burning bush draped the pulpit,
static, only figuratively on fire and definitely not consumed.
It was us who would be consumed if we didn't get saved.
My hat had elastic under my chin, my gloves were white.
I carried a proper handkerchief tucked up my sleeve.

After the third hymn, during the *let us pray* before the sermon,
my mother would palm me a boiled sweet to suck,
taken under cover of bowed head from her handbag
and carefully unwrapped so as not to make a fissle.
I'd sit quiet and behave myself, like a good girl,
daydreaming and imagining swinging hand over hand
around the suspended light fittings and landing
with a simian flourish among the sopranos in the choir.

Time Travelling in Mayo

The wooden bowl has petrified, and each evening
I lie beneath a blanket of mossy green and stone grey,
courage and strength, borrowed from the shoulders

of the mountains; waterfall and rock and cloud.
The swallows remember us and the unpaid piper
tells us he came here twenty years ago and never left.

For days we drive in and out of memory, seconds
spooling back under the wheels, or running
forwards, fuchsia and montbretia along the verges

and it pleases us, this past future perfect continuous —
Do you remember this? — we ask each other.
Here is something that we thought we'd lost.

I have neither the wit nor skill to make sense of it,
I'm just reporting that one moment the clock
has stopped, then suddenly it is much later.

Family Picnic

I think a late summer night would be best,
under a harvest moon in afterglow of sun,
the last real heat of the year. A woollen rug

for us to sit on and there will be tea, of course,
and sandwiches, thin slices of salted tomato,
sliced pan; cold chicken and new potatoes.

When I call them they will come, the hungry ones,
brushing off the soil, straightening their grave clothes.
They won't speak; this is the opposite of speech.

I'll watch them fill their mouths with food.
There will be home-baked buns with raisins in,
raspberries, rhubarb tart, a jug of fresh cream.

They will pack their bellies with what I have provided
and sigh with satisfaction, sated at last, and when dawn
is turning the sky pink with promise, they will go back

to where they came from, lie down and stay there.

The Erne Rushes Through Me

A great clean flood to rinse away
the whole of the tired, wicked world.

A heron guards the dreaming ivory gates,
my eyes have turned the blue of damselfly;
red gilled perch and silver trout,
swim through the ventricles of my heart
and swallows rise from my throat, stitching
my thoughts to the sky: it is as if nothing

bad is happening anywhere: as if
everything in the Garden is lovely.

Beneath the Surface

This stone holds centuries of aching for god,
for winter to pass and the gales to cease.
Sea shifts beneath the wind, silver shiver;
something might rise into the bright November,
aching to be seen, brought into the world of light.

Something swims in the heart, inarticulate:
all the elements — place, image, sensation —
truth waiting to be found, glimmering beneath,
but it comes to nothing, you cannot put your pen
on the nub of it no matter how hard you try.

Ten Days in May

From a Sunday supplement recipe
John makes a sweet rice pudding,
that calls for lots of double cream,
sugar and cinnamon; oven baked.

One mouthful and the taste
takes me straight back,
1974 and the Ulster
Workers' Council Strike.

Uncle Norman bringing churns
of thick unpasteurised milk
uncollected from his farm,
my mother making gallons
of creamy rice pudding,
just to use it up

whilst on the news at six, cars
are burning, bombs exploding.
Maureen Moore aged 21,
is shot dead as she stands
at the corner of Stratheden Street
and a girl of thirteen
steps onto a mine in Andersonstown,
both her legs blown off.

Elegy for Patricia Dorrian

To have your daughter taken
and not know where to find her,
not even the bones of her, body
that you carried in your body,
the bones that belong to you,
her sweet baby bones.

There was searching in sea tides,
boots of cars, sheughs and ditches,
in holes in the ground, in closed faces.
Could the body of a girl be folded
into an oil drum, sealed and dumped
as if rubbish; the most appalling of places
and in your imagination worse even —
but not worse than not knowing.

You wouldn't let them forget her:
you begged for one man with a conscience —
none were to be found. From posters in shops,
on telegraph poles, newspaper articles
each new anniversary, year after ever forever,
your daughter still smiling at the gone world.

Suffering Jesus

Only some cathedrals soar.
Others squat, brutish,
an unrelenting weight
on the shoulders
of the faithful
and the tourists,
as in Seville,

and Christ here
amongst the Inca gold
and glorious
Ferdinand and Isabella,

he looks so tired of dying,
crucified in perpetuity,
never risen.

His are the eyes
of a dog who has
a cruel master.

Mistle Thrush Recurring

Breast narrow with winter, ragged seeker of spring,
Mistle thrush in the garden makes my heart
beat a little harder, and spirit quail a little
at how light he is, how little it might take, a gale,
a hard frost. But he is holding on at any cost,

for he is bull thrush, butcher bird, storm cock,
germinator of mistletoe and though he's deaf,
he speaks in seven tongues, in wild and broken song.
He grows a new set of legs every ten years.
Master of the coppice — Jeremy Joy.

Who knows why some things snag,
out-staying things you should remember.
Tempting to see them as communications,
those bats and birds, foxes, insects, spiders;
but I've never been good at other languages.

Here he is, still bounding into view
just before sleep: who knows, he might be why
tonight I'll dream that I am gowned in ashy brown,
my shoulders bare and the man behind me resting
his hands there — touch of both comfort and desire.

The World Over

Mark calls in, bringing Galena, Baryte and Chalcopyrite
that he's chipped from the rocks around Clandeboye, Conlig,
where the lead mines once stood, where the soldiers
had been got ready for slaughter at the Somme, at Ypres.
He's geologically mapping what's beneath our feet.

I've been reading *Hearts of Down*, the rebels' bodies
left in fields and sheughs and shallow graves,
long mulched back into the soil, only the occasional ball
of musket shot, or a pike head turned up by a plough.
I've been imagining the whole world fed on blood;
the flowers, the good crops that rise up afterwards;
how we all walk on bones and how the indifferent Earth
simply makes use of what comes its way.

As Above So Below

1

By slow degrees
the river stills towards darkness.

Turned to decoupage
in the last of the light, trees

are perfectly reflected in the silver water,
so that up is down, below, above

and the sky and the water know
each other's secrets.

We sit suspended
on the meniscus,

watching the bats stitch
one world to the other.

2

I dream of a slow and ancient
creature

that swims in circles beneath
me

and above me in the deep
wanting

Cailleach

As soon as you arrived
rampaging over the hills,
shaking the stones, lifting
waves of sound and water,
I knew you, and that you
were what was missing
when those women danced
their light-footed goddesses.

Yours was the bellow
I heard in my heart, declaring
life and death the one thing
seen through your one eye.
Tonight you begin to destroy
the things needing to die.
I feel myself folding inwards,
becoming a cave, a cunt.

Time and the Bird

tick-tick-tick-tick-tick
sings the little robin
by the morning river
high days and holidays

and if the heyday
for some thing has passed
don't be fretting about it
there's a wreck around
every corner but sure
here's the morning
and the river

tick-tick-tick-tick-tick
in my head all day
song and clock
bird and me

Cartographer

The transept of my brain's a map,
precisely drawn, indelibly inked
contoured topography of Down,
multi-dimensional and overlaid
with the most meticulous of detail,
everything from where I was conceived
to where I will be buried; where stories
of my identity are told in the intimacy
of street and field, road and every small acre.

Rivers and land and self and time
flow through each other, the Shimna;
the paddling streams; Mountains of Mourne,
the smaller familial hills and fields of farms,
all childhood's dark corners and sunny vistas;
belonging and not belonging; ancient shapes
beneath the bungalow's neatly mown lawn;
saints and settlements, plantations; glacial
drumlins and erratics; the land that formed me.

The six road ends, the four road ends,
the roads we drove, the roads we drive
with views to Scotland, then on around
the Ards peninsula's edge, islands and sky
along Cuan's lough shore — *If you can see
Scrabo Tower, you know you're nearly home.*
Villages I've passed through all my life
on the way there and on the way back,
their names a litany learnt by heart.

Betsy Gray

Killed in the 1798 June Rising of the United Irishmen

Ghost sister, Presbyterian woman, familiar with all my places,
Gransha, Drumawhey, Drumhirk, Saintfield and Ballynahinch.
The men have dressed you since in green silk and given you
a blade of steel so fine the point will bend to touch the hilt.
I see you in more ordinary clothes, moving about your cottage
at the Six Road Ends where history could take any road
into the future, where other futures could unfold; you are
preparing food, greeting your friends, debating by candlelight
the rights of folk to live in freedom from oppression, seeds
of revolt, nourished by the blood of innocents and the winds
from France; I see your Northern coolness and determination.
I feel your hope as the long gathering storm bursts into battle.
A practical woman, setting off to the battlefield with supplies
of cheese and butter and fresh baked bread to feed your lover.

Defeated rebels fled, as you did through the fields of Down;
horror of heads on pikes, mutilated bodies tossed into sheughs
or hung from the windmill's arms on Windmill Hill: a lesson.
At Ballycreen, King's men, Yeomen from Anahilt, caught you,
cut off your hand and stripped you, tore off your earrings,
shot you in the face, left you lying in the green spring.

Sister, you are not one of those angry, implacable ghosts.
The fields of Down are beautiful in June, sweet with grass,
birdsong and blossom; sure just sit a while, remembering.

Bulbs

Last year, in memory of something
or in anticipation of something

(both being loss), I planted
one hundred daffodil bulbs,

buried them one at a time
in the newly turned earth.

Now they are February's yellow
budding of absurd, enduring hope.

Myth Making

It's as if we might have made them up.
Like the night we camped on a hill in Donegal, above
the sea and under a clear sky, watching the Perseids
smear sudden streaks of brilliance across our holiday

and it was like eternity or timelessness or time
or something; our two young daughters, awake
after midnight and watching with us. They both
remember too — I've asked. Even after twenty years,
light is still seared across their retinas; the night when...

Iceland

I went to her with stories and poems
of horses and rain and how I've stood
on the wild edges of my own island
where the land falls off into the Atlantic;
how I've lived with flocks of black birds,
borrowed feathers, dreams, bone-voices.

I found in her a sister dreaming space,
her cold voice a looking glass to step through,
rain to snow, crow to raven, trot to tölt,
river to ice and everywhere her forty
shades of white; light so keen it fills
my eye with blood and every snow storm
with its own song; choirs of glacier and rock,
bone-murmurings on Thingvellir plain,
the language strange, but the sound
familiar, lifted and fluted on the wind.

Then I stood in the rift between continents,
clear and immense; inexorable breath
of a power that knows only its own story.

*

Necrosis shows like a snow cloud
on CAT scan images of his brain; stroke.
Blood fissure deep in the substance splits
the future from itself; my legs trembling
as they trembled in her cold exhalation.

Fearless

Last night I dreamt that we were young again
and loved each other fiercely with our bodies.
It was in the midst of ruin even then,
the roof collapsing in, dust and debris all around.
Ah but we were fearless in the face of time.

While You were Away

To keep the crumpled
iconography of our nights,
I didn't change the sheets;
lay down nightly in the continuing
must of us, tang of sweat and sex
and dreams where we are always
saving each other, so that when
you came home it would be to our
own familiar sweet disorder,
so different to the white, tight
winding of a hospital bed.

Summer Insomnia (is Better than Winter Insomnia)

Four-forty a.m.
and it's either my bladder or my anxiety
that has woken me.
It is almost light on one of the longest days,
the year not yet turned back
and the birds dawn-talking amongst themselves.

Sleep has gone from me,
so I list the things to be done before winter
and trail dark ribbons
of dreams downstairs to the kitchen.
Then, sudden the sun
risen touches me and everything shadow in me
falls into place.

The East Wind May Have Fallen in Love with Me

The night wind from the sea comes gently
through my bedroom window, cool
on my face and breasts and though
I hear it bluster, gust and prowl outside,
when it enters my room it has a lover's touch.

Mare

I am not an obedient or dutiful woman
I never come when I'm called
when I'm hungry I eat
when I'm thirsty I drink

but I'm thinking of the herd of horses
kept from water for three days
then released; the stampede
to the river to be slaked at last.

I'm thinking of those five mares
who when The Prophet sounded
the battle horn, the call to war,
turned back despite their thirst.

These are the Foundation mares
the daughters of the wind
that bred the twelve Royal mares
that bred the winners, their genes

splicing with the three stallions —
faithfulness mingling with pride
duty with self-determination, perfect
combination for passing the post first.

*

I have dwelt in the small universe
of the womb before the world,

felt the power of the womb to expel
into the first sorrow and the first joy,

the abandonment of being: being.
I have been the universe for you.

The circle of the belly, the world,
the life, the mystery of love.

Have you ever heard the soft sound
of a mare whickering to her foal?

What whip will be laid to its back,
what race will it win or lose?

*

Scanned in foal, month after month
her belly became heavier, swollen
until her teats began to fill
and drip with milk; but as more time
went by and no foal came, we saw it was
a phantom that she'd grown, replacing
the clustered beginnings she'd lost long ago.

When most afraid for you, daughter, I think
of her lost embryo. I'd take you back into myself,
every cell, each chromosome. I'd have you back,
before birth, before conception, all your future
still ahead. I'd hold you as an imagined thing, safe.

Home Ground

Ferns lodge the wall; foxglove and mullein
spike through stones; something starred
with dark blue and yolky yellow flowers
creeps through the hedge and climbs.

Horseradish un-tidies the lawn; planted
by birds, trees colonise flower beds; buddleia
blown by the wind to stony crevices, roots
and blossoms, as once, imported, it followed

the railway lines, using the pull of air
from trains to escape from the big houses,
make its way across the countryside.
So it is that exotics become weeds.

I read of a couple who became
lost amongst the rhododendrons.

Untitled

Old horse warms his bones
in the first sun; on his back
he carries winter.

Not Metaphors
For Claire

I do not accidentally come across them
in misty fields, or in old gateways,
I'm aware of where they are,
day in, day out and though always
astonished by the centuries in their eyes,
the grace and beauty of their being,
I also know how much they piss and shit.
I've wheeled thousands of barrow-loads
of dung to the muck heap.

My horses need fed, groomed, shod.
They strain tendons, cut themselves,
get ulcers, viruses, mud fever
and need the vet; colic during the night.
Are they warm enough, safe enough?
Is that one losing weight,
or this one's sacroiliac flaring up?

My horses are schooled and taught
to carry themselves properly, work
through from behind, maintain a light
contact, meet a jump on the right stride,
bascule to perfection; leave the poles up.
That's a lot of work for me and my horses
and sometimes we make mistakes —
fall and get hurt; actually hurt.

Dawn Crows

As if a nest of feathered darkness
had waited there all night to break
against the window pane.

Irrevocable Things

We lead him to the chosen spot.
A bright day, without clouds,
autumn sun still holding its heat.
He trusts us; we've never
given him reason not to trust us.

The sky-blue drug goes in,
we see him feel it hit
and then we watch helpless

the violence of his falling and terrible
tumbling over himself, his desperate
lurching refusal to stay down though
unable to stay up; it goes on forever,
until he's prone at last and Claire
puts her hand over his eye and
he gives in to the shuddering darkness.
A bullet finishes it.

It has dragged the heart from me;
I want to cry: *Wait horse, wait,*
come back,
we'll do it better, it was a kindness
that we meant.

All the regret for every hurt I've ever caused,
sadness for every thing I've ever lost,
is pouring through this rent, that wound,
his drawn-back lips, his emptied eyes.

Essence

When the vet had packed away her gun again and gone
and the carcass had been winched onto the flatbed lorry
and removed, Claire took the hose to rinse away the gore —

told me
afterwards
his blood smelt
like him.

Solitude

It's hard to get used to the shape.
I have become clumsy, accident prone,

missing the last step, banging
my shins, knocking things over,

as if the edge between me and the physical
has blurred a little, become more tentative,

as if I'm no longer sure where the world ends
and I on my own begin, upright and solitary.

*

So many headstones worn to nubs in the long grass,
no memories left, only the ghost shape of a passing,
almost nothing; it is very peaceful amongst the long-dead,
no one grieves for them, their names are on no one's lips.

*

The stone breathes so slowly
and the birds sing so softly
and the sea is so far below

*

The gust that comes sudden over the hill
would take the legs from under you, like a Pooka,
it would take you on its back to the edges of cliffs,
scare the wits from you, before leaving you down
where you started from, unharmed, but different.

*

When I see a horse rise from the sea and come ashore,
moonlight flowing over its flanks like water, I will be ready
to throw a handful of earth at it so it will stay with me.

Just to be Sure

No warping should be done on Thursdays.
Black Thursday comes once every seventh year.

Whoever wears a coat woven
on Black Thursday
will not have long to live.

No one knows which Thursday it is,
so every Thursday should be let pass.

Prey

This summer past, day after day, I watched the buzzard
rise from her stand of trees to hunt; watched her describe
her wide effortless circles, as a wheel set in motion, turns.

This autumn night she has gyred silently above my sleep
so that now at four a.m., I lie awake beneath her dream
and the small, secretive animal of self, trembles.

Return

Why are the horses so long without coming,
And let me suffer so much

Kaspar Hauser — The Wild Child of Europe

Like the viola d'amore, our heart strings lie
below the heart strings of the horse
so that we harmonise through resonance,

and there is truth that lives outside of time
in vivid dream; Raskolnikov's little sorrel beast,
the boy who kissed her dying eyes and lips,

memory perhaps, of when we were not the centre
of the universe, the locus of its consciousness,
not master, owner: we could yet set down the axe.

Vaslav Nijinsky dances the war in Saint Moritz
in front of the aristocrats; he dances *frightening things.*
Finished, he declares: *The little horse is tired.*

Nietzsche, weeping in the Piazzo in Turin, weeps
for the beaten horse, the beaten self: *Sing me a new song.*
If I could remember where the bones were buried,

I would dig them up, the wings of scapulas, the skulls of air,
the golden saddle cloths; reconstruct the horses,
the black horse and the white horse and the horse of fire.

Archive Film — Franz Reichelt — The Flying Tailor

1879 - 4th February 1912

We see him black and white,
standing on the ledge, first
platform of the Eifel Tower

one hundred and fifty feet
above Parisian streets,
despite the pleas of friends

and onlookers: an overstuffed
bat or a badly knitted toy,
swathes of material swinging

beneath his outstretched arms.
We see him doubt, hesitate, step
back and forward, back again

then forwards over the edge and
there's nothing graceful in his fall
or impact, nothing we don't expect —

except for the almost negligible milli-
second of suspension when we
remember the miraculous.

Will for Flight

When the owl came through the night and landed
on the ladder of my ribs, I felt her heart beat hard
into the hollow, felt the strength it takes to hold to air

and my heart rose through the darkness,
joining its musculature with its desire

Devinish Island

Not a hint of monk amongst these stones,
no shiver from the bones beneath my feet.
The round tower is empty, pointing at nothing,

nothing is left of prayer or toil or loneliness.
The waterbus leaves one group of tourists onto
the jetty, picks up the ones who've been, seen.

I rest myself on the graveyard wall and House
Martins skim my skull in happy circles, a wing
span away; chirruping, chittering with laughter.

Apology to the Pike I Didn't Mean to Catch

Invited to throw a line into the water, I did,
but honestly, I never expected you
to take the bait; once you'd done that
I had no alternative but to reel you in.
You fought, bending the rod right back
unto itself, running for the reeds,
thrashing against the insult of the hook,
not giving in until exhausted, and even then.

You smelt of river, dank and green,
and drowning. I saw your teeth.
Our eyes met, predator to predator
on the river bank. My hands shook.
Set again into the flow, you swam back
to your proper place in the undertow.

Rathmullan and Back via Letterkenny

On the way out, we are accompanied by
a crippled Connemara pony, a shotgun,
and a tiny nebulous foetus, no bigger
than an idea. On the way back
they've been joined by a honeymoon hotel,
a dead pug and a teenage girl with a bottle
of blue WKD. They float and rattle along
behind us like balloons and tin cans
tied to the back bumper of a wedding car.

Malediction

I blame my mother

the wicked fairy at the conception
you'll see

she said to me
when you're a mother you'll understand

so the curse is passed on

In the Breeding

Old Paddy always kept a couple of horses,
as if it wasn't a proper life without a piebald
or two in the scrubby field behind his house
and a bit of wheeling and dealing in horse flesh.

He's long gone — it's his son now,
fifty-five-year-old Young Paddy,
the mechanic, showing us photos
on his smartphone screen
of the Irish Draught mare and colt
he got for standing out of the light,
or the scrawny skewbald in foal
to a good stallion, or the warm blood
who jumped at a metre-twenty
before it did a tendon and sure
it might come sound again yet.

Stone

His companions, a little cast-iron flying pig
with stumpy wings and a brass dragonfly,
for twelve years Buddha has sat, eyes closed
legs crossed, hands held cup-shape in his lap.

I have watched him through this time, most patient
and unperturbed of creatures in this stone incarnation,
a perfect spring-perch for the crows, who carry twigs
and horsehair in their beaks, rest on him a moment
before their onward lift to build their chimney nests.
He doesn't mind the white-shit crown that runs down
his face, across his eyelids; rain will wash it off again.
Winter snowfalls cap his head and cape his shoulders,
gather on his thighs, he does not shiver-shift beneath.
Summer sweet-peas curl their tendrils round his feet,
mossy autumn furs him green among the fallen leaves
and he is neither disturbed nor pleased, seated outside
my kitchen window, whilst inside, I grow less steady.

Barcelona Market

That little langoustine, fallen from the counter
and inching its way along the water runnel —
as if it could find its way back to the sea.

East Down Foxhounds Parade

They split in waves to cast for scent, feather
the ground, coalesce into to the one beast-body
of the pack, tails like flags above an ancient army,
faces alert, confident. They know what they're for.

Something carnivorous in my blood responds —
the beauty of these bred-for-purpose dogs,
strong limbed, strong jawed and single-minded
killers, companions to hunters on horses;

but when the pack gives tongue and the Master
blows the *gone away*, my vixen heart shudders.

Everything Stopped

Stopped still as stone
in the long grass,
the fox watches me
watching him.
His coat
dark with rain.

I am the first
to look away
and when I turn back
he's gone
and the sky returns
to falling.

Ghost Story

Settle yourself, keep still
and let the rattling clack itself to a shape.
Let the bones of it sit beside you in the dark;
eventually it will speak.

Keep quiet, don't interrupt,
just listen to the bone-voice and its story
which is not the story you thought
it might have been.

When it has gone again
lean into the silence of absence, the space
it has left you with; then light a candle
and take up your pen.

ACKNOWLEDGEMENTS

I would like to thank the editors of the following magazines and anthologies where some of these poems, or versions of them, first appeared: *Poetry Ireland Review*; *Salzburg Poetry Review*; *The North Magazine*; *Not Very Quiet, Australia*; *The Honest Ulsterman*; *Abridged Magazine*; *Skylight 47*; *North West Words Journal*; *Coast to Coast to Coast Journal*; *Bangor Literary Journal*; *Nobel Dissent & Watch the Birdie* (Beautiful Dragons Press); *Female Lines: New Writing by Women from Northern Ireland* (New Island); *Washing Windows? Irish Women Write Poetry* (Arlen House); *Reading the Future: New Writing from Ireland, 250 years of Hodges Figgis* (Arlen House); Project 365+1 (Australia); *Metamorphic: 21st Century Poets Respond to Ovid* (Recent Work Press). The poem 'Irrevocable Things' won the 2014 North West Words Poetry Competition.

I would also like to thank the ACNI for a Support for the Individual Artist award; and the Irish Writers Centre for a residency in Cill Rialaig.

Thanks to my poetry buddies, the 'Old Daffs', and to Emma Must and Stephanie Conn. Particular thanks to Damian Smyth, who has been a constant support and inspiration over many years. Thanks also to Jo, Angela, Debbie and Diana for their steadfast friendship; and to my husband, John and children, Claire and Jannah, for all their love and encouragement.

MOYRA DONALDSON is a poet and creative writing facilitator from County Down. She has published seven collections of poetry, including a Selected Poems, and her awards include the Women's National Poetry Competition, The Allingham Award, Cúirt New Writing Award, North West Words Poetry Award and the Belfast Year of the Writer Award. She has received four awards from ACNI, including the ACES award in its inaugural year.

Moyra has been widely published in magazines, journals and anthologies in Europe, Australia and the USA, and her poems have been featured on BBC Radio and television, as well as on American national radio and television. She has also read at festivals in Europe, Canada and the USA.

Moyra has been involved with other projects, including a collaboration with photographic artist, Victoria J. Dean resulting in an exhibition and the publication *Abridged 0 -36 Dis-Ease*, and a collaboration with Wexford artist Paddy Lennon, *Blood Horses*, culminating in a limited edition publication of artworks and poems.